# PRESENTS

# THE ULTIMATE GUIDE TO

# TIKTOK

# 2023 EDITION

INDEPENDENT EDITION UNOFFICIAL

Published 2022.
Little Brother Books Ltd, Ground Floor,
23 Southernhay East, Exeter, Devon, EX1 1QL

books@littlebrotherbooks.co.uk | www.littlebrotherbooks.co.uk

Printed in China. Xuantan Temple Industrial Zone, Gulao Town, Heshan, Guangdong.

The Little Brother Books trademark, email and website addresses and the GamesWarrior logo and imprint are sole and exclusive properties of Little Brother Books Limited.

PARENTAL ADVISORY RECOMMENDED

# THE STORY so far...

It might feel as though TikTok has always been one of the main players in social media, but it's still a bit of a newbie. Find out how it all began!

## TikTok started life as two separate apps

called Douyin and Musica.ly. Musica.ly launched in 2014 and quickly started gaining followers and creators. It was a platform for anyone who wanted to show off their talents, whether it was dancing, singing, lip-syncing or comedy. Two years later, tech company ByteDance launched Douyin. Eventually, the two platforms were merged and relaunched as TiKTok.

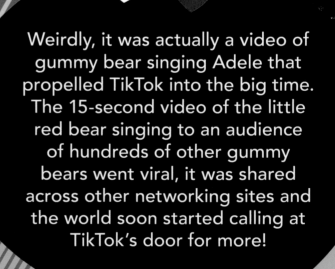

Weirdly, it was actually a video of gummy bear singing Adele that propelled TikTok into the big time. The 15-second video of the little red bear singing to an audience of hundreds of other gummy bears went viral, it was shared across other networking sites and the world soon started calling at TikTok's door for more!

In February 2019, TikTok hit 1 billion downloads. So far, the TikTok app has been downloaded 3.5 billion times.

In November 2020, Charli D'Amelio was the first TikToker to reach over 100 million followers!

When the world went into lockdown in March 2020, many celebrities turned to TikTok to showcase their own dancing and lip-syncing skills. The app also became a great way to keep people entertained while staying indoors.

# TIKTOK
## The Basics

**If you love scrolling through TikTok, but are a bit unsure how to start making your own videos, you've come to the right place!**

### 1 Know what you like

Are there certain **videos and styles** that you **love?** Start thinking about what you are **drawn to**, and what you would love to have a go at. Are you a dancer? A comedian? Want to talk about books you love or TV shows you are obsessed with? Jot down some ideas as you scroll.

### 2 Practice

No matter how many times you watch a video, making one can feel very different. **Practice what you want to do** in front of the mirror before you record.

### 3 Don't be afraid to delete!

And we can't stress this enough, you **can delete** as many times as you like until you are happy! Remember, if you can't quite get something you are happy sharing – you can always **try something else.**

## 4. Safety check

Make sure there is **nothing in the background** of your video that could make you unsafe – or cameos from people who don't want to be on the internet!

## 5. Final decisions

Before your video is uploaded, you will get the **chance to allow comments**, allow stitching and to allow duets. This is totally **your decision**, so make sure you do what makes you happy. Remember, you can always filter words that may be upsetting or triggering for you (check page 64 for how to do this!)

## Upload step-by-step

1. When you are happy with your video, press the + button and upload the video from your library (or record it right there).

2. Next, you can add music. If you know the music you want you can search for it using the search bar, or TikTok may suggest some music for you – depending on what you upload

3. Along the right-hand side of the editing screen, you will see a list of icons where you can add effects, record voiceovers, add stickers and captions.

4. Once you are happy with your video, tap 'next'. The last screen is where you can add a short description of your video, tag friends and add hashtags to your creation. It is also where you can alter the security of your video, who is allowed to see it and use it. You can also automatically share it with other social media apps at the same time if you have them linked.

5. Once you have finished, tap on 'Post' and your video will be added to your page.

# TIKTOK
## Health and Safety

Just like any social media platform, TikTok is the most fun when it is safe to use! Luckily, your favourite app also has some amazing safety features.

### Go private

Set your account to 'private' so that only your followers see your videos. This feature is perfect if you are feeling a bit shy about who sees the stuff you post.

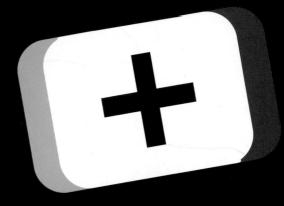

### Eye spy

Remember, if your account is public it means that anyone can view it across the world. Always check your videos for private information that might have accidentally crept in. Can you see your address in the background? Or the name of your school?

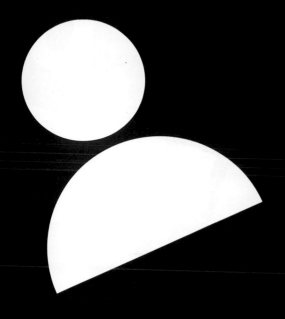

## Restricted mode

If you are worried about seeing something upsetting, flip on **restricted mode**. This will filter out some of the nastier videos out there. Just head to the **Digital Wellbeing section** on your profile.

## Watch those DMs

**Direct Messaging** is only available to users aged 16 and over. If you receive a message from someone you don't know, it is always best to **delete and ignore**. If they continue to message you, you can head to their profile and **block them**. If you would rather no one contacted you through DMs, you can switch it off all together!

## Remember

Never speak to anyone you do not know online and talk to a grown-up if you see or read anything upsetting.

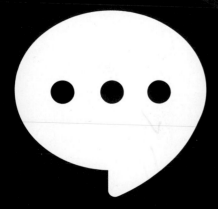

From Charli D'Amelio's TikTok profile page

## Introducing
# CHARLI D'AMELIO

**OVER 120 MILLION followers**

Despite still being a teenager, Charli is the most-watched person on TikTok. Her choreography, lip-syncs and lifestyle videos have been watched over 10 billion times!

## Meeting her idol

Charli has said that one of the reasons she loves to dance is because of music legend Jennifer Lopez. When she was asked to star in a TikTok with her idol to promote the NFL Superbowl, she was blown away. Dreams do come true!

## Keeping up with the D'Amelios

In 2021, Charli and her family debuted their very own reality TV show, *The D'Amelio Show*. The show followed the family as they learn to deal with Charli's new found fame.

## In the family

Charli's sister Dixie has a TikTok account, too! With 57 million followers, Dixie is one of the most-watched people on the internet. She has also released 6 singles and won the Kids' Choice Award for Favourite Social Music Star.

## Award winner

Charli's TikTok content is officially award winning. She won Breakout Creator at the Streamy awards in 2020, as well as Favorite Female Social Star in 2012 and Favorite Female Creator in 2022 at the Kids' Choice Awards.

## What's next?

Charli has her hands full. She has written her own book, designed bedding ranges and stared in music videos. Charli and Dixie also star in their own reality show *Charli Vs Dixie*, completing crazy challenges to see which sister comes out on top.

### OVER 10 BILLION likes

> **You just have to be authentic. You can't fake a smile. You have to do what you actually enjoy.**

*https://www.youtube.com/watch?v=poS7rZ7-_RU

## TikToker facts!

Birthday: **01/05/2007**
star sign: **TAURUS**
from: **NORWALK, CONNECTICUT, USA**
TikTok style: **LIP-SYNC AND DANCE**
Followers: **139 MILLION**
Likes: **10+ BILLION**

From Charli D'Amelio's TikTok profile page

Introducing

# KHABY LAME

OVER
## 134 MILLION
followers

Khaby doesn't need complicated choreography or the latest releases to send his videos viral – all he needs is a ridiculous life hack and his super-expressive face!

## Just... why?

Kahby shot to fame in 2021 after losing his job in the Pandemic. Using the stitch and duet features, Kahby cleverly lambasts life hack videos, showing how they could be done with half the effort.

## Judge Lame

Khaby has become so well-respected in the social media world that he has been asked to be a judge at the first-ever TikTok short film awards at the swanky Cannes Film Festival.

## Pet patrol

Even the best TikTokers need a little help from time to time. Luckily, Khaby's pet pooch, Skippy, is always on hand. From watching gymnastics to doubling up as a napkin – Skippy is one loyal TikTok pup.

From Khaby Lame's TikTok profile page

## Soccer superstar

When footballer Manuel Locatelli completed his long-awaited transfer from Sassuolo to Juventus in August 2021, the Italian club asked a familiar face to help launch his arrival on social media. Khaby appeared in the famous black and white kit, performing his trademark hands-out gesture, before transitioning into the midfielder.

## Boss man

Not content with being one of the funniest, most-liked people on social media, Kahby is now rubbing shoulders with fashion's elite. Having signed a deal with Hugo Boss, he has filmed campaigns with Hailey Bieber and Kendall Jenner!

## You're hired

Khaby had lots of jobs before he became TikTok famous. He wshed dishes, was a waiter and was a bricklayer, too!

OVER **2 BILLION** likes

*I have been making videos since I was child. I always had this thing where I loved to make people smile.*

*Source: https://www.youtube.com/watch?v=txckLNyPcIY

## TikToker facts!

Birthday: **9/3/2000**
star sign: **PISCES**
from: **BORN IN SENEGAL, NOW LIVES IN ITALY**

TikTok style: **LIFE HACK SHAMING**
Followers: **134.1 MILLION**
Likes: **2+ BILLION**

From Khaby Lame's TikTok profile page

From Khaby Lame's TikTok profile page

# SOCIAL Search

ANSWERS ON P71

Can you find all of these words hidden in the grid?

```
L N Y O O E O F E D D N O I N
E L Y R O P C O M E D Y D T D
K I C R E A T O R R E O O L N
I P O I E C D O O I Y Y I T W
N S C O N T E N T N N N P E G
S Y V I D E O U T O D E I R L
P N I N E F U N N Y A A C O I
I C R A R O D A N C E S I U Q
R F E O F I F T E E N C W T Z
E T L N E R I O R L F R E I E
R N O D A E P T T F T O O N R
O C T S T I K T O K O L C E P
U E T I C N N D M C E L R S L
N R U S D L I N I R N R R K L
Y C I J O T O M Y S R L F X Y
```

**Tick** these words off as you find them.

- Comedy ☑
- Content ☑
- Creator ☑
- Dance ☑
- Fifteen ☑
- Funny ☑
- Inspire ☑
- Lip-sync ☑
- Routine ☑
- Scroll ☑
- TikTok ☑
- Video ☐

# YOUR TikTok Handle

Can't think of a cool name for your account or fancy a refresh? Read along the charts to see what your handle could look like!

| Your birth month | The first part of your handle |
|---|---|
| January | JJ |
| February | Love |
| March | M-bot |
| April | Spring |
| May | Gemini |
| June | Ray |
| July | Sunshine |
| August | Summer |
| September | Mr/Miss |
| October | Pumpkin |
| November | Autumn |
| December | Frost |

| Your Birthdate | The second half of your handle |
|---|---|
| 1-5 | 100 |
| 6-10 | Lightening |
| 11-15 | Superstar |
| 16-20 | King/Queen |
| 21-25 | Daydream |
| 26-31 | 123 |

# SPOT THE Difference

Take a look at these images of Khaby Lame. Can you see 6 differences between them?

2-7

From Khaby Lame's TikTok profile page.

2-7

**Colour** in a heart when you spot each difference.

18

From Khaby Lame's TikTok profile page.

**Colour** in a house when you spot each difference.

ANSWERS ON p76!

19

# MOST POPULAR VIDEOS Top 10!

These videos have been played billions of times and their view count just keeps growing!

**1**

## Zach King

### MAGIC BROOMSTICK 2.1 BILLION VIEWS

Officially the most-watched user-generated video on TikTok was made using an electric skateboard, a mirror and a set of fake legs! Yep, we're sorry to say that magician Zach wasn't really riding a broomstick in his billion-viewed vid!

From Zach King's TikTok.

# 2 Zach King

## MAGIC CAKE
## 966 MILLION VIEWS

Zach is back with his second entry into the top ten watched videos of all time – and for a good reason. This video starts simply enough, with Zach pouring water into a glass. What happens next is so hard to believe, we understand why viewers have watched It over and over again. Zach takes out a knife and cuts into the glass, revealing it to be a delicious-looking chocolate cake!

From Zach King's TikTok.

# 3 Zach King

## BEST HIDING SPOT
## 953 MILLION VIEWS

Yep, he's made the list a third time! To be honest, we can see why. This mind-bending trick would have Alice in Wonderland jealous. The video sees Zach trying to find a place to hide when he decides to step through his bathroom mirror (helped by his reflection on the other side).

From Zach King's TikTok.

# 4

## Bella Poarch

## M TO THE B
## 679 MILLION VIEWS

The video that launched Bella into the TikTok big leagues. It might not be the most technical video or use the latest trends, but it showed Bella's personality off perfectly. It also happens to be TikTok's most-liked video of all time with 55 million likes!

From Bella Poarch's TikTok.

# 5

## Zach King

## WET PAINT 659.5 MILLION VIEWS

What can we say? He's just so watchable! Especially this looped video that you could watch over and over again without realising. Here, Zach is innocently painting a corridor when an office worker gets covered in paint.

From Zach King's TikTok.

# 6

## Jamie32bish

## NELLY FURTADO 392.9 MILLION VIEWS

It's short, it's sweet and it inspired a whole load of duets. Jamie now has millions of followers thanks to his bathroom dancing vid.

From Jamie32bish x's TikTok.

# 7

## Daeox

## CUTE BABY: 391.3 MILLION VIEWS

Sometimes all your TikTok feed needs is a cute, smiling baby and, with nearly 400 million, this could possibly be the best of the lot. Big eyes, chubby cheeks and a megawatt smile. What's not to love?

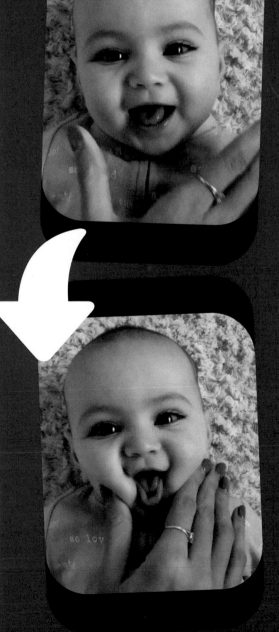

From Daeox's TikTok.

23

# 8

## Khaby Lame

### HOW TO GET OUT OF A CAR 350 MILLION VIEWS

He might be one of the most-followed people on TikTok, but he's only just made it into the top 10. This video features a pointless stick-on car mirror for people who don't know how to open the window!

From Khaby Lame's TikTok.

# 9

## Billie Eilish

### FACE WARP 347.2 MILLION VIEWS

When Billie joined TikTok it was obvious she would be popular, but no one expected her to blow up with her very first video! This funny vid of Billie using the face warp filter is now one of the most-liked and most-watched videos on TikTok.

From Billie Eilish's TikTok.

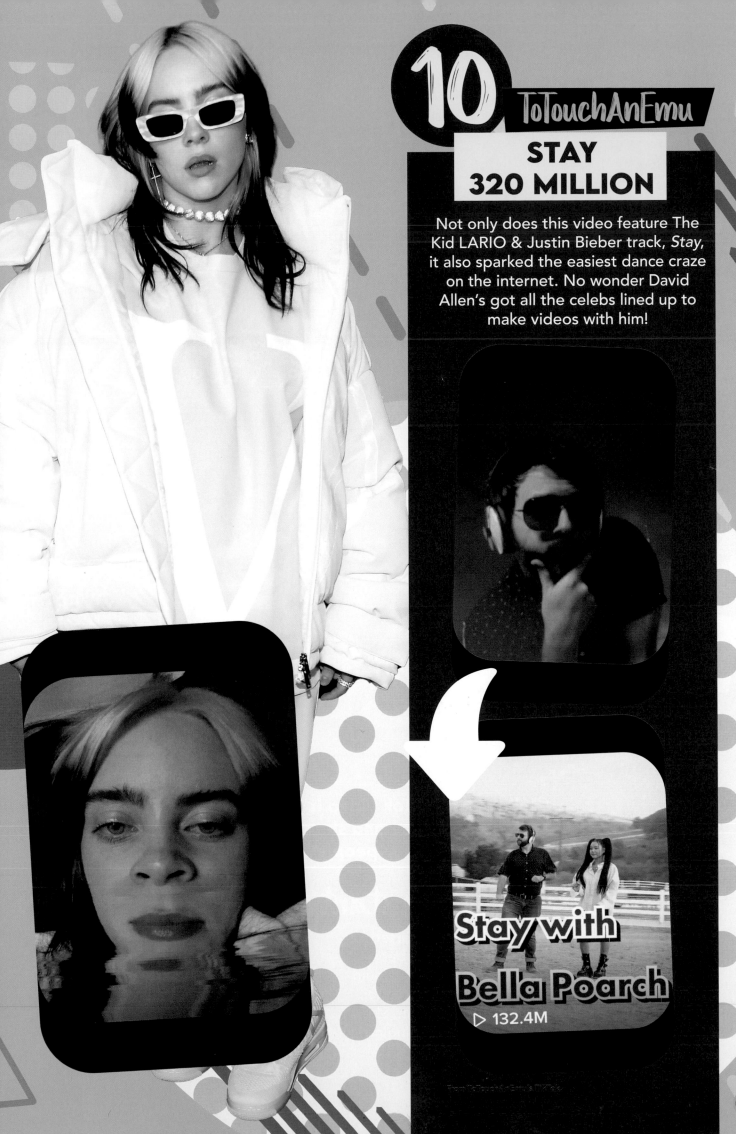

# 10 ToTouchAnEmu

## STAY
## 320 MILLION

Not only does this video feature The Kid LARIO & Justin Bieber track, *Stay*, it also sparked the easiest dance craze on the internet. No wonder David Allen's got all the celebs lined up to make videos with him!

**Stay with Bella Poarch**

▷ 132.4M

From ToTouchAnEmu's TikTok

Introducing

# BELLA POARCH

**OVER 89 MILLION FOLLOWERS**

Bella's first TikTok video is still one of the most watched videos of all time and she's still one of the most-popular people on the site!

## Singing from the start

Although Bella has only just started her music career officially, she has been singing from a young age. Bella would secretly enter talent shows at school, singing Beyonce songs, and win. She collected 34 gold medals for singing all before she even thought of downloading TikTok!

## Seeking a superhero

Bella has an awesome talent for cosplay, but she would love to turn play into reality by starring in a Marvel film. She even has some experience to back up her application – she studied combat training for weeks as preparation for one of her music videos!

## Llama love

One of Bella's constant companions is her plushie alpaca, Paca. Paca has starred in many videos with Bella and even has his own Instagram account and a deal with a clothing company!

From Bella Poarch's TikTok profile page

## Croc champ

In one of Bella's videos, she listed Crocs as one of her top-10 favourite things (her alpaca came top, naturally). She has become so well known for her love of the squishy sandals that she is now a brand partner.

From Bella Poarch's TikTok profile page

## Time to chill

Bella might be one of the most well-known faces on social media, but she would much rather be at home than out living the celebrity lifestyle. She loves writing and meditating at home and spends the weekends with her big brother.

## OVER 2 BILLION LIKES

> I want to take care of alpacas. Alpacas can be by themselves. They're independent and I see myself in them.

Source: https://www.cosmopolitan.com/entertainment/celebs/a39355047/bella-poarch-tiktok-new-music/

## TikToker facts!

BIRTHDAY: **09/02/1997**
STAR SIGN: **AQUARIUS**
FROM: **BORN IN THE PHILIPPINES, NOW LIVES IN SAN FRANSISCO**
TIKTOK STYLE: **LIP-SYNC, DANCE, COSPLAY**
FOLLOWERS: **89.1 MILLION**
LIKES: **2+ BILLION**

From Bella Poarch's TikTok profile page

Introducing

# ADDISON RAE 😊 🖤🖤

OVER **87** MILLION FOLLOWERS

Addison is the fourth most-watched TikToker in the world. Her popularity has turned into acting jobs, beauty ranges and superstar best friends!

## Film star

Addison was cast in *He's All That* a remake of 90s film, *She's All That*. The film became Netflix's most-watched film in the week of its release and has led to more acting offers!

## Move over Gary...

Before TikTok came calling, Addison wanted to be a sport's journalist. She studied sports broadcasting at university and hopes one day to carry on her dream!

## Beauty in the bag

Addison often posts make-up tutorials on her channel. She doesn't shy away from talking about skin problems and break outs, and loves sharing tips on how to get certain looks. It wasn't long before she launched her own range of make-up, skin care and accessories!

From Addison Rae's TikTok profile page

## Keeping up with the Kardashians

Addison met reality star Kourtney Kardashian as Kourtney's son is a huge fan of Addison's. Now, the two are confirmed 'besties' posting videos together and working on projects.

## Parent power

When their daughter started to gain millions of followers, mum Sheri and dad Monty also decided to get in on the TikTok game. Sheri has close to 14 million followers, while dad is not too far behind with 5.4 million.

### Addison's full name is Addison Rae Easterling

## OVER 5 BILLION LIKES

"Staying mentally healthy has been a really big accomplishment for me. This is a lot, and sometimes I think about wanting to give up. But then I remember that I got where I am today."

*https://www.glamourmagazine.co.uk/article/addison-rae-tiktok-glamour-cover-interview-2021

## TikToker facts!

**BIRTHDAY: 6/10/2000**
**STAR SIGN: LIBRA**
**FROM: LOUISIANA, USA**
**TIKTOK STYLE: LIP-SYNC, DANCE, FASHION & BEAUTY**
**FOLLOWERS: 87.4 MILLION**
**LIKES: 5+ BILLION**

From Addison Rae's TikTok profile page

From Addison Rae's TikTok profile page

# CRISS Crossed TikTok

Test your TikTok knowledge by answering the questions and completing the grid.

ANSWERS ON p76!

## Across

4 Surname of TikTok legend, Brent

6 Putting moves together to music

8 You know you've made it when your likes hit over a...

## Down

1 Michael Le's little brother

2 Charli's big sister

3 The TikTok star who's totally 'Lame'

5 The platform for longer videos

7 The type of video tricks created by Zach King

From Michael Le's TikTok profile page

# THEY GOT The Moves

Dance is a huge part of TikTok, so to be the most popular dancers on the platform is quite an achievement! Check out the accounts that are dominating dance!

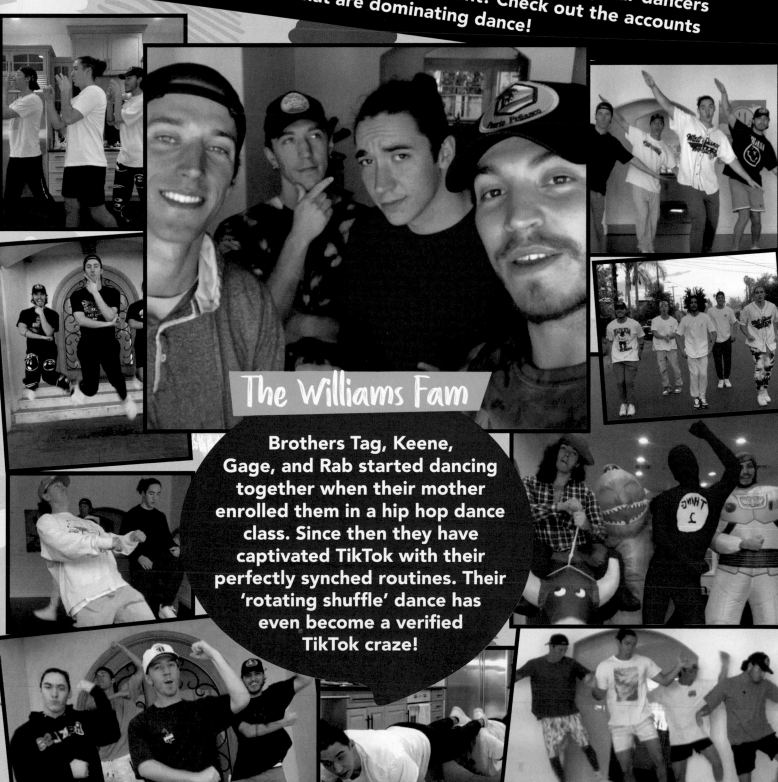

## The Williams Fam

Brothers Tag, Keene, Gage, and Rab started dancing together when their mother enrolled them in a hip hop dance class. Since then they have captivated TikTok with their perfectly synched routines. Their 'rotating shuffle' dance has even become a verified TikTok craze!

Images from Williams Fam TikTok page

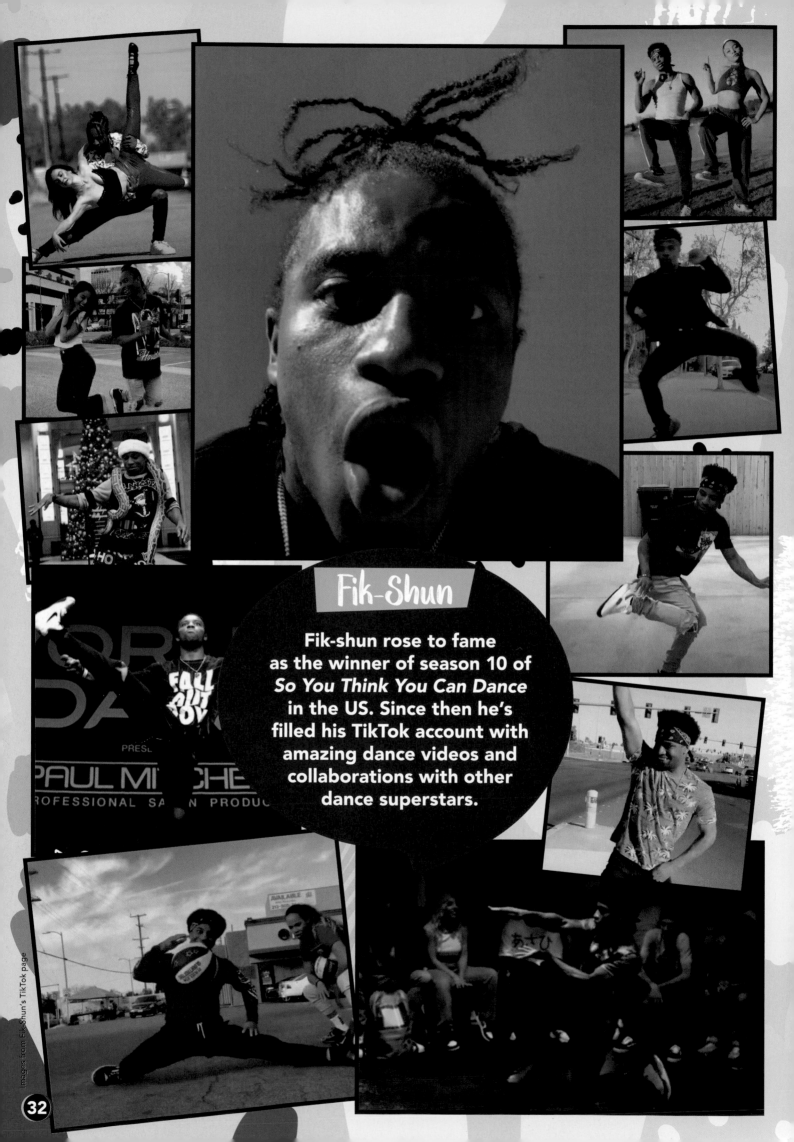

## Fik-Shun

Fik-shun rose to fame as the winner of season 10 of *So You Think You Can Dance* in the US. Since then he's filled his TikTok account with amazing dance videos and collaborations with other dance superstars.

**Right Now Dance**

**Blow Up Dance**

# Dytto

**Dytto (real name Courtney!) began uploading videos to YouTube in 2014. Her 'Barbie girl' dance was picked up and shared thousands of times and revealed Dytto's incredible robotoc moves. Since then she's appeared on dance shows as a contestant as well as a judge!**

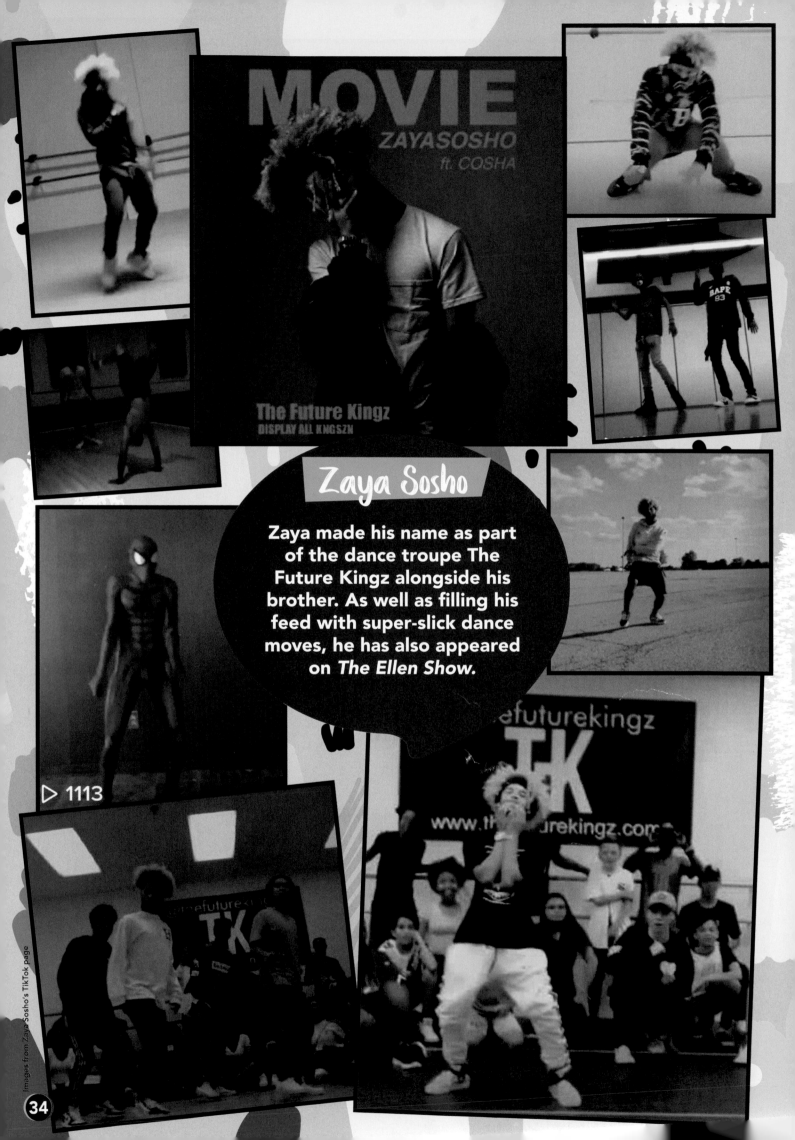

MOVIE
ZAYASOSHO
ft. COSHA

The Future Kingz
DISPLAY ALL KNGSZN

## Zaya Sosho

Zaya made his name as part of the dance troupe The Future Kingz alongside his brother. As well as filling his feed with super-slick dance moves, he has also appeared on *The Ellen Show.*

▷ 1113

thefuturekingz
TK
www.thefuturekingz.com

Do The Juju

## Phil Wright

Not content with being a world-famous choreographer to the stars, Phil has dominated TikTok too! He is the inventor of the 'Parent Jam', challenging kids and their parents to learn and perform dances together!

# TOP Tracks

Music is one of the most-important parts of any TikTok video. Whether it's the soundtrack to a trending dance or the backing to an on point lip-sync, these songs have now officially entered the TikTok hall of fame.

**1** **Love Nwantiti Remix**
CKay ft. Joeboy & Kuami Eugene

**2** **Infinity**
Jaymes Young

**3** **To the Moon**
Jnr Chio, Sam Tompkins

**4** **Pope is a Rockstar**
SALES

**5** Do it to it
ACRAZE ft Cherish

**6** Toxic Pony
ALTÉGO, Britney Spears & Ginuwine

**7** Astronaut in the Ocean
Masked Wolf

**8** Beggin'
Måneskin

**9** Adderall (Corvette Corvette)
Popp Hunna

**10** Stay
The Kid LAROI & Justin Bieber

# HOW TO Lip-Sync

Whether it's your favourite track, synched by your favourite TikToker, or a re-make of a 90s sit com – lip-syncing creates the best videos. Here's how to do it!

## 1 Research!

First up, decide what sort of video you would like to make. Do you want to lip-sync to a music track or a spoken word track? Next time you are scrolling through your feed, take note of the audio you would love to try out. You can even tap on the audio and add it to your favourites.

## 2 Get started

Once you are happy with your choice of audio, rehearse it a few times in the mirror, then tap the plus button at the bottom of your home screen. Flip the camera round to face you.

## 3 Background choices

Remember to think about what is behind you. Do you want a plain background or something that goes with your audio? If your video is all about you, frame your video so there is little background at all.

## 4 Pick your sound

Tap on the musical note at the top of the screen. Here you can select the audio you want to use. Once chosen, click on the pair of scissors icon to edit the audio down if needed. You should now see the name of the audio at the top of the screen.

## 5 Action!

Once you tap the red record button, your audio will start to play and you can create your lip-sync. Don't worry if you don't get it right the first time – you can re-record until you are happy.

## 6 Edit & go

When your audio clip finishes, you will be taken to the editing screen where you can add filters, words, stickers and all the usual TikTok additions. Click the red arrow button to write in your description and add hashtags.

## Remember

Don't forget to credit the original audio creator in your description!

# TIKTOK Jargon Buster

If you are new to TikTok, there may be a few words you hear that you don't understand. Don't worry, we've got you...

## MOOTS

Moots are people who follow you, who you follow back

*Example: This one is exclusively for my moots!*

## IB

Short for 'inspired by'. This is great if you are doing a version of someone else's video. It's usually followed by tagging the person you were inspired by.

*Example: This song IB Billie Eilish*

## FLEX

To flex means you are bragging about something – and you know it.

*Example: I can touch my nose with my tongue. Weird flex, I know.*

## CHEUGY

In short, this is the opposite of being on trend. It can be used when creating funny, ironic or silly videos.

*Example: I know these trainers are totally cheugy but I kind of like them!*

## FIRE & LIT

If someone comments that something is fire or lit – it means they really like it!

*Example: Your skills are lit!*

## NO CAP

Used when you want people to know you are being totally serious about something.

*Example: I just saw Justin Beiber in Starbucks. No cap.*

## STORYTIME

This is usually used as a hashtag to signal that your video is telling an anecdote.

# (NO) BONES DAY

A bones day is a day when you are full of energy and ready to attack the day. A no bones day means you would rather be hiding under a duvet. It all depends on what Noodle the pug decides to do that day when his owner @jongraz picks him up. If he stays upright, it's a bones day!

*Example: Today is going to be a bones day. I can feel it!*

## BUSSIN

Used to describe something that is really good, usually food.

*Example: This burger is bussin!*

## DC

*Dance credit:* Use this when you have learnt someone else's choreography for a video.

## PFP

Short for profile picture.

*Example. You should make that your pfp!*

## RT

This one is taken straight from another social media platform, Twitter! It means that you agree with something so much, you would retweet it (if you were on twitter)

## SHEESH

Use this one wisely as it can mean that you are impressed by something, or you don't believe it just happened. Team with an emoji to make your meaning clear.

## TEA

Tea simply means gossip, or something interesting. It's the perfect hashtag for a storytime video!

*Example: Listen up everyone, do I have some tea for you!*

# RECORD Breakers

TikTok is one of the biggest platforms in the world, and it shows no sign of slowing down. Check out these official world-record-breaking stats!

## Most comments

This award went to **Minecraft fan** account @meqs. They racked up **10.9 million comments** in January 2022 asking their followers to 'comment for a cookie'.

## Most viewers for a live TikTok performance

With **5.5 million views** and counting, **Ed Sheeran's live concert at Portman Road** (home of Ipswich Football Club) officially broke records in June 2021.

Images from Flighthouse's TikTok page

## Most Followed Brand

**Flighthouse** create original videos with everyone from established TikTokers, to pensioners and big-name brands. They have **28.3 million followers.**

## Most-followed actor

**Will Smith** took the title in January 2022 with nearly **65 million followers** – making him the 6th most-popular person on the whole platform!

## Most followed music group

Of course, it had to be **K-Pop megastars BTS** with **49 million followers!** They also broke another world record by becoming the fastest account to reach 1 million followers.

From Zach King's TikTok profile page

## Introducing ZACH KING

OVER 120 MILLION FOLLOWERS

Zach was amazing the internet for years before TikTok made him a megastar. Let's find out more about this mind-bending filmmaker.

### Starting young

Zach started making videos at the age of 7. He bought himself some editing equipment at the age of 14 and never looked back.

### Love film

Zach studied filmmaking at university and even created online training sessions for other filmmakers to help him pay for his tuition.

## Famous friends

His videos have become so well-known that some of the biggest stars in the world want to be in them. Zach has made videos with Jeff Goldblum, Tom Brady and Selena Gomez.

From Zach King's TikTok profile page

## Posting Potter

One of Zach's most-famous, most-liked videos is of him riding a broomstick, apparently on his way to Hogwarts. He also made a follow-up video showing how the effect was created.

## Screen idols

Zach admits to being slightly obsessed with directors George Lucas, Steven Spielberg, and Peter Jackson. He would watch behind-the-scenes footage from their famous films to see how the magic was made.

### OVER 10 BILLION LIKES

> "No one thinks the magic is completely real, people know there is some trickery going on, but there's an aesthetic to it that feels real."

* https://www.digitaltrends.com/web/illusionist-zach-king-interview/

## TikToker facts!

**BIRTHDAY:** 4/2/1990
**STAR SIGN:** AQUARIUS
**FROM:** OREGON, USA
**TIKTOK STYLE:** ILLUSION
**FOLLOWERS:** 67.5 MILLION
**LIKES:** 850 MILLION

From Zach King's TikTok profile page

From Zach King's TikTok profile page

From Dixie D'Amelia's TikTok profile page

## OVER 57 MILLION FOLLOWERS

## Introducing DIXIE D'AMELIO

**Following her little sister's lead, Dixie has now joined her in the top 10 of most-loved TikTokers!**

## Finding strength

Despite Dixie's first singles being streamed millions of times on Spotify, she often finds criticism hard. "Music's always been a part of my life and I enjoy it and I love sharing creativity with people. I just want to do what I love and share it with the people who love me."*

## The Early Late Night Show

Dixie hosts her own TV show on YouTube where she interviews celebrity guests (including her sister!) The show started life in the family's living room, but was upgraded to a totally sweet studio for the new series.

* Source: https://www.smh.com.au/culture/music/dixie-d-amelio-a-tiktok-superstar-tries-to-segue-to-a-music-career-20211018-p59116.html

## Billboard love

It's no secret that Dixie and Charli love their mum. For Mother's Day, the two stars got together and bought her a billboard with a poster that told their mum just how much they loved her.

## Solo star

Dixie has always loved to sing, and in June 2020 she finally released her first single, *Be Happy*. She has since collaborated with Demi Lovato, Wiz Khalifa and Rubi Rose. Her debut album is expected in late 2022!

## Fashionista

Dixie loves getting dressed up as much as she loves spending her days in an oversized hoodie and tracksuit bottoms. Along with sister Charli, she has collaborated with brands like Hollister and Puma to create and promote the stye she loves.

From Dixie D'Amelia's TikTok profile page

From Dixie D'Amelia's TikTok profile page

## Award winner

Dixie won a Kids' Choice Award for Favorite Social Music star in 2022!

### OVER 3 BILLION LIKES

> "I feel like TikTok was the first app to show a natural side, you could post in a messy room and show a naturalness and, like, mistakes."

*Source: smh.com.au/culture/music/dixie-d-amelio-a-tiktok-superstar-tries-to-segue-to-a-music-career-20211018-p59116.html

From Dixie D'Amelia's TikTok profile page

## TikToker facts!

**BIRTHDAY: 12/8/2001**

**STAR SIGN: LEO**

**FROM: CONNECTICUT, USA**

**TIKTOK STYLE: SINGER AND LIP-SYNC**

**FOLLOWERS: 57 MILLION**

**LIKES: 3+ BILLION**

From Dixie D'Amelia's TikTok profile page

# DANCE Phenomenon's

Have you noticed how certain dances always seem to pop up on your feed? Find out more about these iconic moves!

From Totouchanemu's TikTok profile page

From Shakira's TikTok profile page

## Stay

Take one man, one drone and a The Kid LAROI and Justin Beiber track and what do you get? Possibly the easiest dance craze on the internet. David Allen (@totouchanemu) has now performed his drone dance with musical legends such as Paula Abdul, Jason Derulo and TikTok's own Bella Poarch!

## Jiggle Jiggle

A newbie on the TikTok scene, the 'Jiggle Jiggle' dance has really caught on. Performed to a rap by broadcaster Louis Theroux, it's easy to pick up, silly, and lots of fun (WARNING: This rap is likely to stay in your head for a long time!)

From Kausha campbell's TikTok

## I Like To Move It

Who knew that a griup of animated lemurs could be responsible for one of TikTok's classic dance hits? Unlike most TikTok dances (that are usually performed in one spot) this one moves forward continually and requires energy and acting skills, too!

From Debzlin's TikTok

## Domino

The cutest dance for couples, siblings and friends! Performed to Jessie J's *Domino* it requires what the professionals call 'arm-ography' and practice. It's also a good one for transition videos!

From Daniel Myers TikTok

From Katie Feeney's TikTok profile page

## Iko Iko

Another TikTok classic, the *Iko Iko (My Bestie) (feat. Small Jam)* dance needs at least one other person (although it has been performed with many more!) It's a fun, sweet dance perfect for beginners and guaranteed to leave a smile on your face!

## Beggin'

So, once you've mastered the classics, time to move on to something a little more complex. This Beggin' dance was created by @katiefeeneyy, and although at first glance it may look tricky, once you have the moves down it's a really fun one to get on your feed!

# BEAUTY Queens

From extreme transformations to honest reviews, these beauty experts have everything you need to know!

## 1 Abbey Roberts

Abby started posting make up videos in 2019 when she was 17. Her third video blew up and she now has millions of followers! Abby's style has always been to create extreme make-up transitions, as well as giving tips to her fans. She's now branching out into music, too!

From Mari Maria's TikTok.

## 2 Mari Maria

Mari is a Brazillian make-up influencer who started out on YouTube before moving on to shorter videos on TikTok. She mixes make-up tutorials with hair styles, dances and even some cute cameos from her family!

## 3 Mikayla Nogueira

Mikayla is all about make-up. Just like Mari, she started out on YouTube and moved to TikTok after she helped her mother with a school project. Mikayla loves to give honest reviews about viral trends and new products.

▷ 2.7M

*From Mikayla Nogueira's TikTok.*

## 4 Hyram Yarbro

Hyram is an Hawaiian influencer who is passionate about skin care. His fun and honest videos are packed with tips on how to keep your skin healthy, as well as the best products to use regardless of how fancy they are!

▷ 398.8K

*From Hyram Yarbro's TikTok.*

## 5 Danielle Marcan

Danielle has loved make up ever since she was 12 years old, searching YouTube for tutorials to copy. She fills her feed with celebrity copy-cat looks and product reviews. She has even been featured in advertising campaigns!

▷ 391.6K

*From Danielle Marcan's TikTok.*

## 6 Bretman Rock

Bretman teams beauty videos with amazing backdrops from his home in Hawaii. As well as fun make-up looks, Bretman creates funny videos, lip-syncs and shows off his fashion looks. He's teamed up with brands such as Urban Decay and Morphe.

# ALL ABOUT Style

Take a look at your favourite TikToker's early posts and you'll see something they have in common – they all tried lots of different styles before finding their vibe. What will yours be?

## DANCE

Scroll through any user's home feed and you won't get far before a dance video turns up. From super, high-speed choreography to the mega-simple Siren Dance, learning dance moves to a short piece of music is one of TikTok's most-popular things to do – and almost anyone can have a go!

## TRANSITIONS

A transition video is used to quickly change from one thing to another. It could be an outfit change, a make-over or even home decoration. There are lots of fancy editing techniques to research, but one of the easiest ways to transition between shots is with the hand technique. Simply approach the camera with your palm flat until it makes the screen black. At the start of your 'reveal' video, place your hand over the camera again and slowly take it away.

## LIP-SYNCING

Lip-syncing is the art of moving your mouth in time to a backing track. It could be singing, rap or a piece of audio from a film or TV show. It's a super-popular way to have fun, make people laugh or pay tribute to your favourite track. Lip-syncing can take a while to get right, so make sure you listen to your piece of audio lots of times before you begin. Practice your facial expressions and any dance moves in a mirror before hitting record.

## STORYTIME

Storytime videos do exactly what they say – tell a story! They are usually a head and shoulders shot of the storyteller and sometimes have graphics over the top to make the story pop.

If you have a story to tell, write it down first in a fun and imaginative way. Try to learn the story by heart before you film (or try a teleprompter app). TikTok videos are quite short, so if you have to tell your story in more than one video, make sure you say which part you are telling in the description and the video itself! Check out Leslie Mosier's storytime video on the top celebrities who have met Doug her famous pug!

# ANIMAL Lovers

Okay, so Charli is great and Brent is pretty funny, but are they as cute as these famous furry TikTokers?

From Floofnoodles' TikTok.

## Floofnoodles

Not only does this **fabulous ferret** have possibly the best name on the internet, she also has over **17 million followers!** Floof loves a cooking video, hanging out with her ferret pals and dancing to the latest TikTok-trending tracks.

## Jiffpom

**Jiffpom** is an adorable **pomeranian** who has won the hearts of millions of followers (20.6 million to be exact!) Jiffpom can usually be seen hanging out in a hoodie at his favourite coffee shop, but he's also starred in TV adverts and a **Katy Perry's** *Dark Horse* music video!

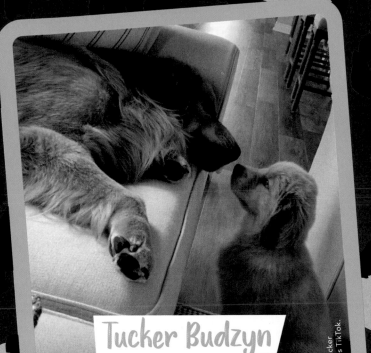

From Tucker Budzyn's TikTok.

## Tucker Budzyn

**Tucker** is one of the most-recognised pups on the internet. The **fluffy golden retriever** has over **10 million followers** on TikTok and his fans can't wait to see what he does next. Handily, Tucker's followers always know what he is thinking as **his thoughts appear on screen**. Recently, Tucker has been joined in his videos by his own puppy, Todd, meaning there is twice as much cuteness to watch!

From Bunny's TikTok.

## I Am Bunny

**Bunny** has gained his **7.3 million followers** by showing of his **awesome conversational skills.** Using a clever matt of buttons where different words are played when pressed, Bunny can tell his owners what he needs and how he is feeling.

From Chase, Millie and Skye's TikTok.

## Chase, Millie and Skye

These three **pampered kitties** have made a simply perfect start to their TikTok careers. With nearly **10 million followers** watching as they cuddle up with their owners, take trips in the car and **chill out with a feline spa day.**

## Otis the Turtle

Despite sharing the limelight with some other reptilian friends, **Otis** definitely takes **centre stage** on this account. One video of him hiding behind a tape measure has racked up nearly **200,000 views!**

## Peanut the Squirrel

**Peanut loves** two things above all else. **Food, and his long-suffering human!** Together they **bake, work out** and **clear out all the nutshells** peanut loves to hide around the house.

## Big Boy Bru Bru

**Bru Bru** is a **French Mastiff** who does not like to be moved from his **favourite place on his human's bed.** With nearly **200,000 followers**, this big chap is fast becoming one of TikTok's good boys!

## Cool Cat Lou

**Lou** can usually be **spotted cruising the streets in his jeep**, meeting the locals and occasionally getting **stopped by the police!** Luckily, they always want a quick selfie before Lou can head back out on the road!

# TIKTOK
## Fame and Followers

TikTok trends, family footage and behind-the-scenes peeks makes these celebrity accounts some of the most-followed in the world!

From Will Smith's TikTok profile page

## Will Smith

**72 million followers**

Will Smith is one of the most-famous actors on the planet, so when he joined TikTok it was almost guaranteed that he would gain millions of followers. However, Will's love of camera trickery and some incredible stunts (like standing on top of the world's tallest building) have secured his place as the number one actor on TikTok.

## Jason Derulo

**52 million followers**

Jason is having fun on TikTok. As well as having loads of his tracks as TikTok favourites, Jason and his family regularly post funny videos of everyday life, including asking his followers what they should name their new baby!

## The Rock

### 52 million followers

Who doesn't love Dwayne 'The Rock' Johnson, right? The wrestler-turned-actor has gained millions of followers with his playful videos, family insights and behind the scenes footage. His most-popular video sees The Rock and BFF Kevin Hart all dressed up as an elf and Santa – ready for the holiday season!

## BTS

### 50 million followers

They've conquered the music world, now they are coming for TikTok. K-Pop's biggest band fill their feed with cute dance snippets and music. Their most-popular video shows all seven members dancing to their world-wide hit, *Dynamite*.

## Kylie Jenner

### 40 million followers

The reality star has gained millions of followers on TikTok by posting videos of her family life and business career. As well as cameos from her famous siblings, Kylie often shares moments with her little girl, Stormi and baby Wolf.

## Selina Gomez

### 41 million followers

As well as posting clips from her music videos and collaborations, Selena fills her feed with funny lip syncs, dances with her sister and having fun with her friends. No wonder she has millions of dedicated followers!

From Spencer X's TikTok profile page

From Spencer X's TikTok profile page

# Introducing
# SPENCER X ♡ ♡ ♡

**OVER 120 MILLION FOLLOWERS**

### The beatboxing marvel has famous fans and big plans for the future!

## Musical beginnings

Spencer was introduced to music at Middle School in New York. He played around with the drums and trumpet, before his friend taught him how to beatbox. From then on, Spencer was hooked and started to research techniques!

## Boy in the band

Spencer has been part of not one, but two acapella singing groups. The first was called The Midnight Ramblers who even auditioned for a TV singing show!

## Famous friends

His beatboxing talents have been recognised outside the social media world, too. He has teamed up with Alicia Keys as well as Sean Kingston!

From Spencer X's TikTok profile page

## Viral hit

The video that propelled Spencer into the limelight was called One Beatboxer, 14 Genres and it featured Spencer's talents in everything from dubstep to trance – with a bit of dolphin throw in!

From Spencer X's TikTok profile page

## YouTube and beyond

Spencer wants to take beatboxing even further by making longer videos on his YouTube channel. He wants to collaborate with musicians who might not have come across his skills before, as well as actors and comedians.

**OVER 10 BILLION LIKES**

> " I knew this was my purpose because it made me feel happy. Eventually, beatboxing became my best friend! "

*Source: https://www.youtube.com/watch?v=LRIgEZyPSt4

From Spencer X's TikTok profile page

## TikToker facts!

BIRTHDAY: **20/4/1992**
STAR SIGN: **ARIES**
FROM:
**NEW YORK CITY, USA**
TIKTOK STYLE:
**BEATBOXER**
FOLLOWERS: **55 MILLION**
LIKES: **1.3 BILLION**

From Spencer X's TikTok profile page

From Michael Le's TikTok profile page

From Michael Le's TikTok profile page

## Introducing
# MICHAEL LE

OVER **51** MILLION FOLLOWERS

Michael's smooth moves, flair for comedy, and of course, his little brother, have made him one of the most feel-good accounts to follow on the internet!

## In the house

In 2020, Michael moved into a 9000 square foot mansion with four other social media stars. Together they formed Shluv House – a collaboration of innovative content creators. The house is the perfect place to shoot videos, and yes, Jonathan and Tiffany are frequent visitors!

## Dance history

Michael has been dancing since the age of four, and was one of the first dancing stars on TikTok, in fact, he first joined the platform in 2016 when it was know as Musica.ly. Before that, Michael had his own YouTube channel, showing off his dance routines and posting dance tutorials.

## Oh, brother (and sister)!

Michael has two brothers and a sister, but his most-frequent co-stars are his sister Tiffany and little brother Jonathan. Both Tiffany and Jonathan can bust out the moves and have started to get their own fans!

From Michael Le's TikTok profile page

## Up and down

Some of Michael's most successful videos involve an escalator. Whether it's dancing with a pal on opposite sides, or screaming Shakira songs in front of startled shoppers, Michael makes full use of any moving stairways on offer!

## Did you know?

According to Michael, Maiko comes from the Asian way of spelling Michael.

**OVER 1.4 BILLION LIKES**

> I knew from middle school that I didn't want to be a person that just had a nine to five.

*Source: https://www.forbes.com/sites/tomward/2020/10/07/michael-le-is-building-an-empire/?sh=1495c58a6f8f

## TikToker facts!

BIRTHDAY: **19/3/2000**
STAR SIGN: **PISCES**
FROM: **FLORIDA, USA**
TIKTOK STYLE: **DANCE, LIP SYNC & COMEDY**
FOLLOWERS: **51 MILLION**
LIKES: **1.4 BILLION**

From Michael Le's TikTok profile page

From Michael Le's TikTok profile page

# HOW TO BE
# TikTok happy

Social media can be a fun place to discover new things and connect with friends. However, as with any platform, there are things you can do to make sure TikTok remains a safe and happy place to be.

## 1 Screen time

We've all heard of limiting screen time, but there are some strong reasons for cutting back on your phone or laptop time. It is recommended that anyone up to the age of 18 should have no more than two hours a day (unfortunately this does include homework time!). You can set a timer on your phone to tell you when you've used up your scrolling minutes. Having too much screen time can: give you headaches, make you grumpy and interfere with sleep patterns.

## 2 You be you

Just because everyone seems to be doing the same super-complex choreography doesn't mean you have to do it too. If uploading videos of your cat snoring in the sun makes you happy – go for it. If lip-syncing to *Friends* audio clips makes you giggle – get to it. You'll soon find what brings you the most joy.

## 3 Take a break

If you notice you are thinking about TikTok videos or singing the latest TikTok-famous track in your head the moment you wake up – it might be time to take a TikTok Detox. Hiding or deleting the app from your phone for a few days might be the rest you need, plus you'll love it even more when you get back on.

## 4 Follow happy

Who you follow is super-important to keeping you happy and your mind healthy. Really think about how you feel and how your brain reacts to certain content. Does someone you follow make you feel bad about yourself? Unfollow. Do they say things you think are upsetting or mean? Unfollow. It can be someone you know or even a celebrity – if they're bringing the vibe down on your feed, you know what to do! Instead, choose accounts that make you laugh, lift you up and make you feel inspired.

## 5 Blocking and Word Filtering

If you like to upload videos, but worry about your followers being mean, there are two brilliant tools you can use. Blocking is the best way to get rid of anyone online who is upsetting or bullying you. Simply go to their account, tap on the three lines in the top right-hand corner, then scroll down to the block button. Secondly, you can filter out any comments that have certain words in them, so they don't appear. Head to the 'Privacy and Safety' section on your account then: 'Filter Comments'. You can then activate: 'Filter by Keywords' and type in any word you don't want to see in your comments section.

From Brent Rivera's TikTok profile page

## Introducing
# BRENT RIVERA

OVER **43** MILLION FOLLOWERS

**Brent is one of the most-popular creators on social media. His TikTok channel is the place to go for feel-good silliness.**

### Born entertainer

Brent wanted to be an actor when he was younger, and started out in the entertainment business at the age of 10. He first became well-known on Vine before hitting the big time of YouTube and TikTok.

### Turn up the Amp

Brent is part of the Amp collective, a group of content producers made up of friends and siblings. The collective have a great time putting videos together as a group, as well as supporting each other's own accounts.

## Prank-tastic

Brent has become the king on TikTok pranks. From getting friends to dress up as mannequins to having fake fights with his sister – you never know what Brent might get up to next.

From Brent Rivera's TikTok profile page

## Anti-bullying champ

Brent was chosen to be the face of an anti-bullying campaign by fashion brand, Hollister. Brent said that receiving negative comments online opened his eyes to bullying and showed him ways to cope.

## Acting dreams

His dreams of becoming an actor came true when Brent starred in *Alexander IRL*, a film about being cool, making friends and, naturally, social media!

**OVER 1.4 BILLION LIKES**

> *I definitely made a lot of videos, but when I film with my friends, it's super fun.*

Source: https://popentertainment-interviews.tumblr.com/post/617585027400810496/staying-home-with-brent-rivera-by-ari-lafayette-at

From Brent Rivera's TikTok profile page

## TikToker facts!

BIRTHDAY: **9/1/1998**
STAR SIGN: **CAPRICORN**
FROM: **CALIFORNIA, USA**
TIKTOK STYLE: **ACTING, DANCE AND CHALLENGES & BEAUTY**
FOLLOWERS: **43 MILLION**
LIKES: **1.4 BILLION**

From Brent Rivera's TikTok profile page

From Avani Gregg's TikTok profile page

From Avani Gregg's TikTok profile page

# Introducing AVANI GREGG 😊

**OVER 120 MILLION FOLLOWERS**

**The girl with the BEST make-up tips, and a few famous friends, too!**

## Summer school

Avani wanted to finish high school with all her qualifications, but her celebrity lifestyle was getting in the way. So, to make sure she didn't miss out on anything, Avani took lessons over the summer holidays!

## Gym bunny

Avani was really good at gymnastics when she was younger, and we mean REALLY good. Had it not been for an injury on her back, Avani could have reached Olympic levels.

## Best friends

If you've seen any of Avani's videos recently, you might have noticed a familiar face. Avani often teams up with superstar Charli D'Amelio, posting dances and generally having fun and messing about!

From Avani Gregg's TikTok profile page

## What a Gem

Avani has turned her TikTok fame into an acting role in Brat TV's *Chicken Girls*. Avani plays Gemma, one of a group of friends who navigate the tricky world of being a teenager!

## Here For It

As well as posting videos, Avani has had her own TV show! On *Here For It*, Avani interviews fellow social media stars and gives advice to her fans.

**OVER 10 BILLION LIKES**

> "Taking care of my mental health while being on social media and my wellbeing in general, is very hard. That's why I usually take breaks. I will take 3-5 days of staying fully off my phone."

Source: glamourmagazine.co.uk/gallery/beauty-spy-avani-gregg

From Avani Gregg's TikTok profile page

## TikToker facts!

BIRTHDAY: **23/11/2002**
STAR SIGN: **SAGITTARIUS**
FROM: **INDIANA, USA**
TIKTOK STYLE: **MAKE UP, LIP SYNC AND DANCING**
FOLLOWERS: **41 MILLION**
LIKES: **2+ BILLION**

From Avani Gregg's TikTok profile page

# YOUR TikTok account

Use this page to plan your TikTok rise to fame!

## Tik Tok handle

Need inspiration? Head to page 17!

## Your bio

Use this space to sum up who you are in a few short words, E.G. Dogs and dancing – not always at the same time!

## What's your style?

## First five accounts you are going to follow

1
2
3
4
5

## You want to be just like...

## Hashtags you'll always use

## Top five tracks you are going to use

1
2
3
4
5

## Goals for your account

Use this space to jot down what you want from your account. Sharing advice? Making people laugh? Making fun videos with friends?

# WHAT'S YOUR TikTok Destiny?

Answer the questions to see where your TikTok journey will take you!

## 1. How long do you spend deciding what to wear in your video

**A)** A little while, comfort is more important than style!

**B)** No time at all, the video content is stylish enough

**C)** Ages! Your look has to be perfect

## 2. What's the definition of a perfect TikTok?

**A)** Great music and sick moves

**B)** Something that makes you smile

**C)** One that inspires you

## 3. Who's your favourite TikTokker out of...

**A)** The Williams Fam

**B)** Brent Rivera

**C)** Kylie Jenner

## 4. Who would be your dream brand to colab with?

**A)** Nike

**B)** Netflix

**C)** M.A.C

## 5. What would your friends say is your best quality?

**A)** You have loads of energy

**B)** You're great at cheering people up

**C)** You give great style advice

## 6. Which of these jobs would you love?

**A)** Dancer or dance instructor

**B)** Writer or stand-up comic

**C)** Stylist or designer

---

### Mostly As
## DANCE CRAZE SUPERSTAR

When you hear the latest track or see a new dance craze, you've got to get up and try it out! Your destiny is to create your own dance that goes viral and has everyone from The Rock to Prince William vibing along with you.

### Mostly Bs
## CROWNING COMEDY

You love to make people laugh, so you are destined to fill your feed with funny vidoes. Whether it's challenges, lip-syncs or routines, you are here to put a smile on people's faces.

### Mostly Cs
## STYLE ICON

Your dream would be to become the top style TikToker on the planet, drowning in free merchandise that brands are desperate for you to review. Your looks would be copied millions of times!

# BEST OF The Rest

These TikTok stars have millions of followers and cover everything from dance, music, comedy and style. Which ones do you follow?

## Jo Jo Siwa

**41 MILLION FOLLOWERS**
TIKTOK STYLE: LIFESTYLE AND DANCE

In short: Although JoJo is still only 19, she has been in the limelight for a long time, starting out as a dancer and reality TV star, before becoming a businesswoman and judge on the US version of *So You Think You Can Dance!*

## Noah Beck

**33.4 MILLION FOLLOWERS**
TIKTOK STYLE: LIP-SYNC & LIFESTYLE

In short: Like a lot of new TikTok stars, Noah started posting videos during the pandemic as a way of keeping occupied. He's now a fully-fledged TikTok star and is currently dating fellow TikTok star Dixie D'Amelio

## Call me Kris

### 44.1 MILLION FOLLOWERS
### TIKTOK STYLE: COMEDY

In short: Kris Collins has built up her loyal following thanks to a range of comedy characters. From mums to little kids, taxi-drivers and even her own brain – Kris can transform herself into almost anyone, while still being recognisably her!

## Joe Albanese

### 41 MILLION FOLLOWERS
### TIKTOK STYLE: COMEDY & DANCE

In short: Joe is all about having fun, and he's not afraid of looking a bit silly in the process! With the help of his little sister, and occasionally a Barney costume he's gaining followers and seeing just how far he can test his mum's patience!

## The Dobre Twins

### 35.6 MILLION FOLLOWERS
### TIKTOK STYLE: DANCE AND COMEDY

In short: Lucas and Marcus love a challenge, especially if it means one of them ends up looking silly! They team dance videos with pranks, skits and games – often including their older brothers and parents!

## Baby Ariel

### 35.7 MILLION FOLLOWERS
### TIKTOK STYLE: LIP SYNC, MUSIC AND LIFESTYLE

In short: Ariel Martin began her life on social media on Musica.ly in 2015 and has been one of the most-popular internet celebrities ever since. She's fronted her own anti-bullying campaign and even starred in the Disney trilogy *Zombies* as an over-excited werewolf!

# Answers

```
L N Y O O E O F E D D N O I N
E L Y R O P C O M E D Y D T D
K I C R E A T O R R E O O L N
I P O I E C D O O I Y Y I T W
N S C O N T E N T N N N P E G
S Y V I D E O U T O D E I R L
P N I N E F U N N Y A A C O I
I C R A R O D A N C E S I U Q
R F E O F I F T E E N C W T Z
E T L N E R I O R L F R E I E
R N O D A E P T T F T O O N N
O C T S T I K T O K O L C E P
U E T I C N N D M C E L R S L
N R U S D L I N I R N R R K L
Y C I J O T O M Y S R L F X Y
```

2-7

1. JONATHAN
2. DIXIE
3. KHABY
4. RIVER
5. YOUTUBE
6. CHOREOGRAPHY
7. ILLUSION
8. BILLION

# Picture Credits